Plenty of Petals

Counting by Tens

by **Michael Dahl**

illustrated by Zachary Trover

Special thanks to our advisers for their expertise:

Stuart Farm, M.Ed., Mathematics Lecturer
University of North Dakota, Grand Forks

Susan Kesselring, M.A., Literacy Educator
Rosemount–Apple Valley–Eagan (Minnesota) School District

PICTURE WINDOW BOOKS
Minneapolis, Minnesota

Editor: Christianne Jones
Designer: Jaime Martens
Page Production: Zachary Trover
Creative Director: Keith Griffin
Editorial Director: Carol Jones
The illustrations in this book were created digitally.

Picture Window Books
5115 Excelsior Boulevard
Suite 232
Minneapolis, MN 55416
877-845-8392
www.picturewindowbooks.com

Printed in the United States of America.

Library of Congress Cataloging-in-Publication Data
Dahl, Michael.
Plenty of petals : counting by tens / by Michael Dahl ;
illustrated by Zachary Trover.
p. cm. — (Know your numbers)
Includes bibliographical references and index.
ISBN 1-4048-1317-9 (hardcover)
1. Counting—Juvenile literature. 2. Addition—Juvenile
literature. 3. Daisies—Juvenile literature. I. Trover, Zachary,
ill. II. Title.

QA113.D352 2006
513.2'11—dc22   2005021818

Finn was leaving the hospital with his leg in a cast and a vase full of daisies.

ONE HUNDRED petals in the vase.

10 20 30 40 50 60 70 80 90 100

100

Finn gave a daisy to his nurse.
"Nifty!" said the nurse.

4

NINETY petals in the vase.

10 20 30 40 50 60 70 80 90

Finn gave a daisy to the doctor.
"Dandy!" said the doctor.

EIGHTY petals in the vase.

10 20 30 40 50 60 70 80

Finn gave a daisy to the receptionist. "Ravishing!" said the receptionist.

8

SEVENTY petals in the vase.

10 20 30 40 50 60 70

9

Finn gave a daisy to the taxi driver. "Terrific!" said the taxi driver.

SIXTY petals in the vase.

10 20 30 40 50 60

Finn gave a daisy to his mom.

"Magnificent!" said his mom.

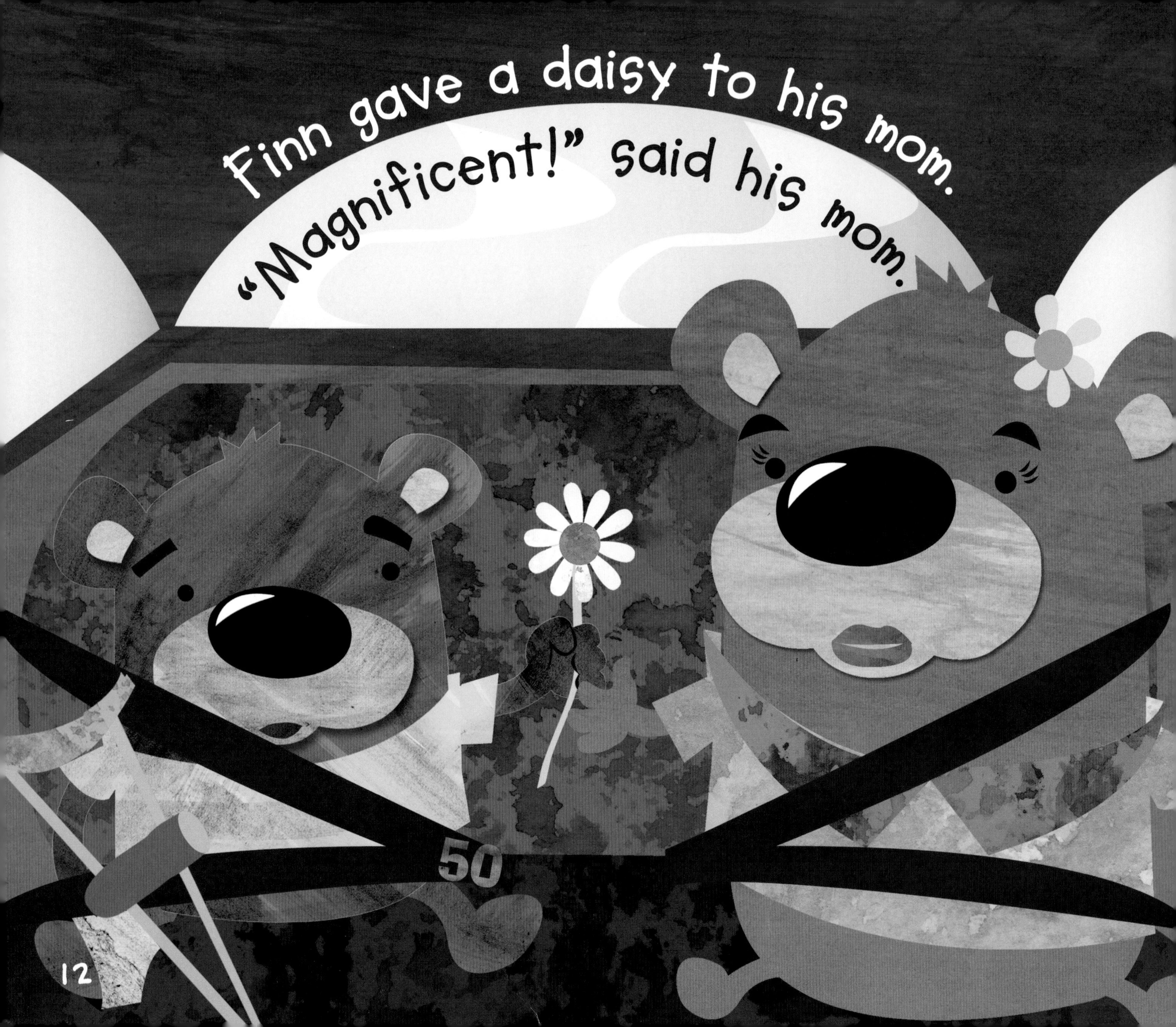

FIFTY petals in the vase.

10 20 30 40 50

Finn gave a daisy to the police officer.
"Pretty!" said the police officer.

FORTY petals in the vase.

10 20 30 40

THIRTY petals in the vase.

10 20 30

17

Finn gave a daisy
to the doorman.
"Delightful!" said
the doorman.

18

TWENTY petals in the vase.

10 **20**

Finn gave a daisy to the neighbor's boxer.
"Bowwow!" barked the boxer.

TEN petals in the vase.

Finn gave the last daisy to his father. "Fantastic!" said his father.

"From now on, I'll only skateboard outside," Finn said to his parents.

Fun Facts

 Scientists believe there are more than 270,000 kinds of flowers.

 Some flowers bloom only at night. These night flowers are pollinated by moths.

 The small leaves on a flower that are directly under the colorful petals are called sepals.

 The word *daisy* means "day's eye." The flower opens up at sunrise and closes at sunset.

 In ancient China, roses were grown and owned only by royalty. If an average person was found with rose oil on them, the punishment was death!

On the Web

FactHound offers a safe, fun way to find Internet sites related to this book. All of the sites on FactHound have been researched by our staff.

1. Visit *www.facthound.com*
2. Type in this special code for age-appropriate sites: 1404813179
3. Click on the FETCH IT button.

Your trusty FactHound will fetch the best sites for you!

Find the Numbers

Now you have finished reading the story, but a surprise still awaits you. Hidden in each picture is a multiple of ten from 10 to 100. Can you find them all?

10—on the boxer's collar
20—on the awning
30—on the mail carrier's bag
40—on the taxi's back wheel
50—on the seatbelt buckle
60—on the front of the taxi
70—on Finn's cast
80—on the doctor's bow
90—on the nurse's pocket
100—on a flower

Look for all of the books in the Know Your Numbers series:

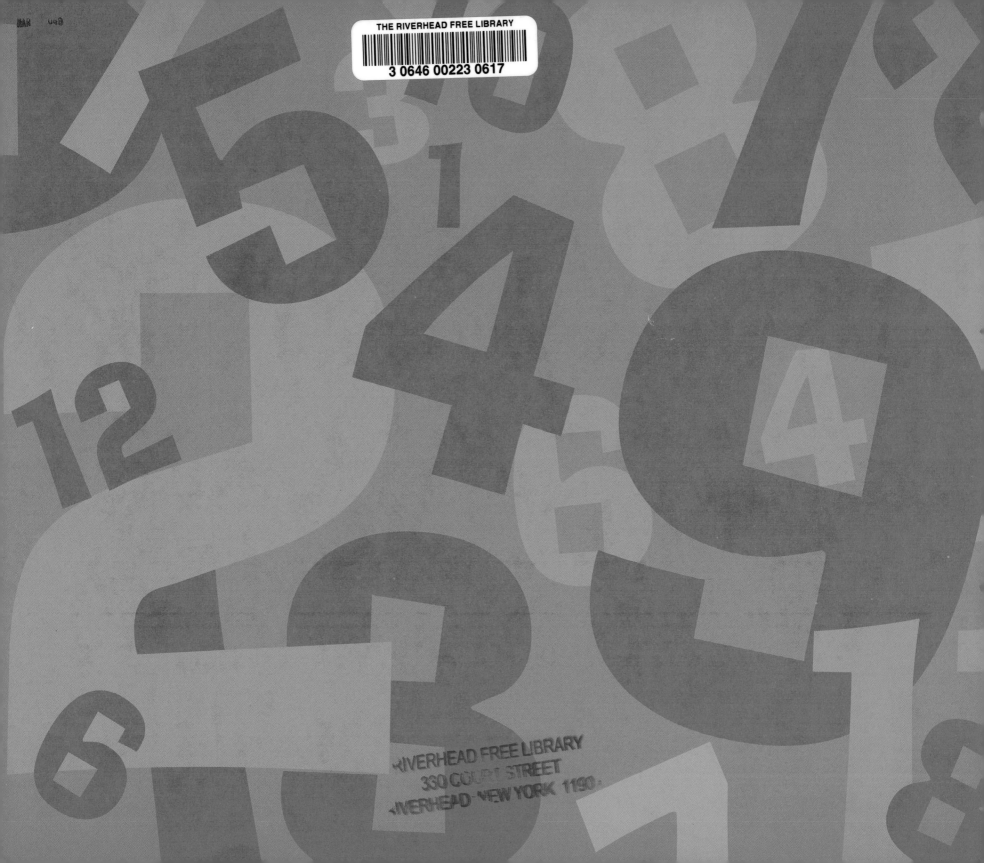